MAXINE BENEBA CLARKE

HOW DECENT FOLK BEHAVE

T0283895

hachette
AUSTRALIA

Published in Australia and New Zealand in 2021
by Hachette Australia
(an imprint of Hachette Australia Pty Limited)
Level 17, 207 Kent Street, Sydney NSW 2000
www.hachette.com.au

  A catalogue record for this
book is available from the
NATIONAL LIBRARY OF AUSTRALIA   National Library of Australia

ISBN: 978 0 7336 4766 6 (paperback)

Cover design by Allison Colpoys
Cover photographs courtesy of Stocksy (2565310, 2381755) and iStock (884971268,
1189598064, 482694831)
Author photo courtesy Nicholas Walton-Healey
Text design by Bookhouse, Sydney
Typeset in 12/16.6 pt Bembo MT Pro by Bookhouse, Sydney
Printed and bound in Australia by McPherson's Printing Group

An artist's duty, as far as I'm concerned,
is to reflect the times.

Nina Simone

CONTENTS

prologue

i said

get the fuck back,
i am warning you:

i've got poetry

their hands were trembling,
their eyes were wild,

and i could smell
their fear

WHEN THE DECADE BROKE

when the decade broke

the stroke of midnight,
december 31, 1999,
       was going to end the world

at the hospital,
       they brought generators in

even the food service staff
were kept till late evening

none of us would get to
           aaaaah,

at the most expensive fireworks on earth,
       lighting up a new century:

if the power cut out,
       we planned to spend armageddon
pigging out on defrosting sara lee
  and handing out the bottled water,
down in maternity

    we would control the food, we joked,
and therefore, everything:

in the new century, we, the workers,
would be king

just like one day
            we'll say

where were you,
on december 31, 2019

– and perhaps more importantly –

who were you
before the decade turned

don't look at me like that,
you know what i mean:

who were you, when thunder was made
            from our protesting children's feet,

when 45,
>   (the then-president
of the united states of america)

had just been impeached

we'll say to young ones:

>   unthinkable now,
isn't it
>   that back then, in this city,
women's bodies were sometimes found
naked, from the waist down;
we would gather in the parks,
for candlelight vigils

that in this very place, the decade
before revolution came,

>   nobody *led*
though four prime ministers

>   rose, and fell;

innocent black folk were shot
      at point-blank range
regularly
across the world,

and often incarcerated
for no valid reason at all

don't avert your eyes from mine

you should know
what this place was:

earth on fire,
from the redwoods of california
to australia's east coast

my god,
      the furnaces
that burned:

in brazil, they lost a good part
of the amazon

the sea drew back,
        and tsunamis lashed out
in samoa and sumatra;
the water rose,
in sulawesi and nagasaki

in the new decade, we will say
        the world
was not always this beautiful way:
in some countries,
  small children starved to death

                every single day

    but that all slowly started to change

and powerful men
were brought to trial

  for heinous acts of hate

we threw them out,
and relegislated

(they'd made the churches
far more powerful
than the state)

for a good while there
we thought we were doomed,

   that it was all just way too late

but the decade turned

the decade turned,
and suddenly,

   we were wide awake

lined along the gun-powdered foreshore,
faces tilted to the sky,

    watching revolution break

generation zoom

in the third week of the pandemic

       schools started closing,
workers were sent home,

and they started to call the youngsters:
     generation zoom

named, of course, for that chat-app
all of them seemed to use:

logging in for facetime,
completing maths lessons online, dancing
tiktok feeds on loop, clicking in
to instanews, and everyone was asking

     what on earth will become
     of whatsapp's children?

  visiting friends
through cracked iphone glass,
and advised to stay away

     from their own mama's arms

who weren't allowed
to warm to touch

cause don't you know
there's a virus going round

and

less is love, baby, less is love

parented
from 1.5 metres away

what hope the future,
when a whole generation
grew up this way:

socially distant
quarantined

     and self-isolated

no giggly schoolgirl notes
tucked into the pockets
    of square-checked tunics

nor the exquisite
stomach churns you used to get
when someone you liked

stood

    close to you

but generation zoom,

they saw the neighbours
from two doors down
put a note in their letterbox
asking if they still had food

generation zoom
streamed bitter fights
      in supermarket aisles
over toilet paper
and baked beans

but they also saw us learn
how to grow the world, from seed;

how the cities, silent
were so beautiful

how, for the first time in so long,

        dad was home:
and he vacuumed, and
forgot to act

    like dinner was his due,

and all the family
were on the same timeframe
in the same house

defrosting bolognaise, and
bickering, and bunking in

elijah's boyfriend
        was finally allowed to phone:

even though mum was
'still confused about the whole gay thing'

cause don't you know
there's a pandemic going on

and
  love is love, ma, love is love

in the end
we'll be okay,
cause generation *zoom*
grew up today:

learning stocks can be lost
as fast as accumulated

that health is wealth
and love is gold

and life

    will find a way

RAIN

RAIN

september

september germinates,
       determined

all sure-quiet-beautiful
       and fern and jade unfurl

in furrows dug with fothergill's

       and hope,
with compost care

september breathes,
and seeds new life

      and at the sunset,

       spring cicadas
form a deafening sonata

       shedding skin to crisp

a spring rebirthing,
in the warming

      evening breeze

oh, september
brings remembering

of fertile earth

      and worm

     of chrysalis,
as swooping magpies

       proud their nests

and cockatoos
squawk fidgeting

         for fruit

here blooms september:
   southern-spring,

the ghost of all this earth,
and what we've lost,
and all we are,

and all we stand

to lose

ancient giants

               we'll say
the summer right before
was blue-green algae

bastard took the bony bream
    and silver perch

reckon it grew from heat
and farming run-off

cyanobacteria is what they said

               we'll say
that very jan we killed
    the murray–darling
shit,
    australia was the hottest place
on earth

riverbanks were
powder-keg with spinifex

    bushfires raged
and the mercury,
it burned

we'll shake our heads
we think it started up menindee,
least that's where the first stories
rolled in from

when darkness fell
the oxy dropped
    below the water

    stillness,

and then
the bodies
    slowly rose

                and they'll be wide-eyed leaning
                forward peeking-through-fingers,
                saying: come on, pop, just tell us
                what happened next?

    we'll whisper
dead fish
putrid-bloated
eyes skull-sunken
    fly-blown all along the retching banks

deflated
  decomposing
ancient giants

there's a picture somewhere here,

we called them *cod*

22

arson

i

the redhead
        on the matchbox
is all charcoal lash

she wears a *do it* smile,

like eve's,
        to adam

ii

most arsonists, they say,
        are men

some of them like to go back

        and watch:

scarlet flickering
in transfixed eyes

or else they dial,
>> to *raise the alarm*

iii

bushfire burns faster
>> when travelling uphill,

than descending,
or on even keel

the spread doubles,

with every ten-degree incline:

flame licks closer
to unburnt fuel

iv

slender-fruit saltbush,
and angular pigface

frosted goosefoot
    and rounded noon-flower

spotted emu plant,

silver mulga

knife-leaf wattle,
and then, the acacia

v

the wind creeps,
        enchanted,

in the footsteps of the fire:
and blows burning leaf litter ahead

the speed of the scorch
wreaks havoc,

        and haste

firefighters: broken,
and bracing

rain

no rain in sight,
  all hot south-westerlies

    spring-tinder

grey smoke, coiled
  around the cowering
sunshine coast

amanda wheezed,
and sucked her ventolin

dad called out
    we're leaving soon,

and wet the roof again,
with hose

mum said

the car's all packed
what are we waiting for?
we had a plan, come on, get in

                              let's go!

in the end
          we left
their wedding photos

packed in cardboard boxes,
                              in the hall

when the fire came,
the four of us just legged it:

grabbed the dog,
got in the car, and drove

rain

dad said
        jen, i think
you might be speeding

 mum snapped back
        well yeah,
of course i am

we were lucky, we got out
and lived to tell the tale

even though we never saw
    our house again

after,
    everything looked really different

the trees were charcoal poles,
                no birds flew by

mum cried amongst the ashes:
kicked charred spoons

where her new countertop once lay

dad's shoulders drooped:
  he bit his lip,
and blinked his eyes, and

               looked away

he said *these fires,*
     they make runways
  of the landscape scars
  we settlers made

mum snapped
      oh, don't start that nonsense,
we just needed bloody rain

fridays

on fridays,

our children are bursting train carriages
backpacked full of hope

wielding placards bedroom-made
from flattened cornflake boxes

and upcycled tomato stakes

on fridays,

our children raise melodic voices
meant for playing tag, or jump-rope

and take to the streets,
in every city,

million-strong,

and begging us
to *know*

in the empty classrooms,

silence echoes
round initial-etched desks

and lockers, left open, spill
crumpled science notes

      on fridays,

our kids are forced
to become *adults*

on the ball court,
  a lone grey hoodie hangs,
               abandoned,
        from the hoop

every week, our children sacrifice
one-fifth of their dreams

      and on fridays,
they become exactly

who we need:

marching
with their arms around
each other's tiny shoulders

and their iphones held up viral-high

they are brave enough
to defy instruction;

sure enough
to face the future,

and smart enough
to know their minds

if they save the world,
                    or not:

        on fridays,
                    our children tried

winter

silence,
   all across the mourning fog
dark winter has descended

birds flee to warmth
from branches, gnarled

and hope

      drifts on the wind

crisp leaves

      once crumbling
underfoot

 lie sodden, in the mud

how bleak the world
both seems,
and is:

cold, settling

in the bones

SOMETHING SURE

dorothy

dorothy down the yellow-brick
lost a lion's share of teeth-grit

she gave away everything she knew

even a chamber
    of a beating heart
to a tin man,
who couldn't feel

all the boys, they got
what they wanted

before the velvet curtain dropped

and we still call her story
        the wizard of oz

something sure

sit down here now baby,
       stop that fidgeting

listen big,
and understand

mama's gotta school you
'bout something sure,
         'fore you grow into a man

now, hannah clarke,
she died today

we don't know her
from soap, it's true

she the one in the papers:
whose ex burn her up,
as she driving the kids to school
(yeah, he pour petrol on three little ones –
and kill them angels too)

hurts my heart to think on it,
so baby, mama needs to know:

that a good man,
   the man you'll grow to be,

         can lead a bad man home

d'you know to say
      nah, don't do that mate
   or
         that's not fucken right,
you heard her, take your hand off her shoulder
and how 'bout you and i call it a night

i know you're young,

            and i taught you well
how decent folk behave

but if the time comes,
every woman is your mama,
            when it come to saving

like if she on the street
and he smell like trouble:

getting right up close,
and in her face

or some colleague in the lunch room's saying
that damn bitch took my babies

if his veins all popping, fists all clenched
and his eyes are still as death

will you call it out,
or call it in now baby,

trust your gut,
and use your head

we women mostly got each other's backs
but sometimes busy, just surviving
set up against the acid throwers
hands–gripped–round–throats
locked doors, and petrol fires

and every two minutes
the state is called

to deal with
domestic violence

but a boy like you
          could grow
to make a difference

          if you try

like if he say
i'm gonna make her pay,

a man like you
could remind him

about the time the twins were born
when he came in late;

          could not stop smiling

saying

    man, her back was arched in agony
but she wasn't screaming ay:
just got our bubs here safely

shit, i won't forget today

see, hannah and them kids
died brutal,

we don't know 'em all
                    from soap,

but it aches my soul to muse on it
so babe, your mama needs to know

that a good man,
exactly the man you'll be,

                    will lead a bad man home

icarus

icarus,
     her father fashioned wings

but he made her flight
a conditional thing

said *don't fly too high:*

baby girl, when you fly,
just don't fly too high

but icarus said *i am*
going to burn

and i might burn,
but i will fly,

and mark my words:

i will see
     every altitude

before i die

me too

there are other women,
who want to say

me too,

but can't:

they sit at home,

minding the children
of women who march,

and hoping to god,

the husbands
of those women

do not
arrive home
            first

my feminism

after flavia dzodan

the local women's march
is pink-dressed,
determined, *alive*

the cheering chanting mass
streams past the inner-sydney sights

a bold sign centre-crowd,
floating up on high, says:
i'll see all you nice white ladies
at the next black lives matter march,

right?

my feminism
is intersectional, or
my feminism
is a lie

half-a-million knitted pussycat hats walk
angry-calm on washington

they chant:
we're women. united.
we'll never be defeated.

my feminism
is the black sister:
white cap; fierce as

– you know the one –

there she is, nonchalantly sucking on a lollipop
while bearing a hand-painted placard that says:
don't forget, white women voted for trump

my feminism
will be intersectional,
or my feminism is done

my feminism
does not feature
in the *suffragette* credit roll

my feminism
is not a scroll
of the places and dates
white women got the vote;

does not holler
across the loud promo t-shirts that say:

*i would rather
be a rebel*

*i would rather
be a rebel
than a slave*

    my feminism
can love emmeline pankhurst
for what she did,

and still roll its eyes
at emmeline pankhurst's phrasing

    my feminism
can respect germaine greer's legacy,
but detest her transphobic ways

    my feminism
will be critical,

and analytical, and
brave

     my feminism
will not reveal itself

as white feminism at thirteen,
queer feminism at twenty-five,
and poc, aboriginal,
first peoples, or disability feminism

if you *identify*, are *ultra-left*,
are *bleeding-heart*, are
so inclined

     my feminism
will always question

     my feminism
must get wise

     my feminism
will not claim that nuance is *divisive*:

all feminism is flawed, but
    my feminism
will try

    my feminism
would not anti-think-piece
beyonce's pregnant glow,
    because
    my feminism
remembers the brown children
bought and sold

    my feminism
slips unseen
through the bars
and razor wire

    my feminism
will amplify
the songs
of the silenced

my feminism

my feminism
is pro-choice,
but does not endorse
lena dunham's abortion wish

my feminism
says termination is not
a girl guide collar pin

my feminism
does not shout down
pro-lifers who shame abortion,
then shame abortion grief, or regret

my feminism
will be kind

my feminism
is complex

my feminism
does not complain
about middle-class childcare fees,
without campaigning

for the women who child care
                on a minimum-wage index freeze

        my feminism
does not go
smashing glass ceilings
at the same time it builds glass walls

        my feminism
will be class-aware,

                or it will have no class at all

        my feminism screams
about equal marriage rights
in the country where i live,

while in the country
of my parents' birth,

corrective rape is still a thing

        my feminism
is fierce

     my feminism
crossed oceans
     my feminism
learned to swim

     my feminism is uneased
by unceded land; was sung
by audre lorde; knows
wilma pearl mankiller

     my feminism
haloed harriet tubman

and signed the statement
at combahee river

     my feminism
says *no woman left behind*

     my feminism
says the strongest will go find her

     my feminism's
the underground railroad out

      my feminism
will ferry us through all the doubt
      my feminism
seeks to lift *all* women up
      my feminism
must be strong enough

      my feminism
is strong,
fierce,
burning,
alive

      my feminism
will be smart,
intersectional
and kind

      my feminism
is truth: that bold sign up on high

it's inevitably flawed,
but will always try

my feminism

      my feminism
can smash glass ceilings
and walls

      my feminism
is wondrous,

and will
    elevate
us *all*

grace

rocking
back and forth,
on the labour ward floor

room blurring,
mind wild with:
hell, i mean, i was so out of it,
i can't even explain
what kind of pain
                that was

but the only thing that mattered
was that they got here sure,

and arrived home whole
every subsequent day:

my children taught me
that feeling never goes away,

that a certain chamber of your heart
will now be occupied
until your dying day;

grace

the enormity of what you are
to each other,
         always

my children taught me
sometimes life happens around you
and at others, through:

a reckoning in, and of, itself
that was birthed,
but does not belong,
to you

that sometimes life arrives
with a solid will
and a treasure map
under chubby brown arm
plants its feet at the top of the slippery dip,
sits down, and flat-out refuses
to walk home from the park

sometimes life
spits baked beans across the kitchen,
tips stewed apple on its head,

then stares up at you
    like it loves you
        more than anyone else on earth

sometimes life wakes you six times a night,
and pees all over the bed

lies down, stroppy, in the grocery store
and all the neighbours stare
while you try to coax it up, gets
nap-cranky at the childcare worker
and is sent home
with a naughty-note

my children taught me

sometimes life
gets up on *exhibition day* at school
and surprises you

with an acoustic version
of *castle on the hill*

sometimes life brings
the whole concert hall to its knees,
    and you can barely believe
it's yours

my children taught me legacy:

my own mother's grace, and her
mother's grace, and her mother's grace,
     and hers

how, despite a world
not made
          for women like us

the ferocity of our love, alone,
will hum our families home

the monsters are out

the monsters are out
the monsters are out

and the women of melbourne,
  we're leaving early again:

sending *are you home?* texts glancing
over shivering shoulders keeping
friends on the line until
the key's in the lock

oh sisters,
  we forgot

jill had only just got off a safe-call;
eurydice texted to say she was almost home;
masa went out for a walk and
  and, well,
aya,
  she caught
the bundoora tram home

so here we are,
holding vigil again:

two-dollar-a-pack-at-coles
tea light candles,

　　　　flame flickering
rage-high

shoulder to shoulder,
　　　　bleeding
against the sobbing
summer light

but most of the monsters
have the same face
as our sleeping four-year-olds

the monsters gave us valentines

some of the monsters
have the other key card
to our shared bank account

the monsters are out
the monsters are out

and oh how we flame,
　　　　against the sobbing
summer light

but when we're done mourning,
some of us go home
                    to die

proximity
for natalina angok

they are the women

whose bodies
    don't quite make front page

carefully measured outrage

    when it happened
they weren't walking home
from a white-collar job
post friday-night drinks

at a bar you recognise

and even if you learned them,
you forgot their names

        after a while

here,
    search the photos

see their smiles

they were mourned
by sliding scale

according to proximity

to —

damn that could have been me

don't remind you
of your sisters girlfriends
daughters selves, or wives

so their faces bleed towards the staplefold
and their killer's state of mind will matter

more than their coloured lives

capital

in grade five,
they bus our children
       to the capital

to the long white building,
high–majestic, on the hill

where the boys mostly learn:

you study hard,
you might well work here
one day, mate

while the girls hang back,
and button their collars:

this place
is where women
get raped

TROUBLE
WALKING

trouble walking

i

what do you mean
you're having trouble walking

it seems self-explanatory,
but i raise
the folded black walking stick
that's been resting
                    across my lap

this must've been going on
for quite some time

why didn't you come and see me
            earlier

in that moment, i am
just another irresponsible ethnic

whose condition has worsened
because they never got help

what on earth
are you people afraid of

the truth is,
to end up here, in the gp's chair,
black pain must be unbearable

the agony
must be greater
than our greatest fear

on a scale of one to ten,
where one is that you can barely feel it,
and ten is –

where ten is birthing a baby,
through a twenty-four-hour labour, i say,
on panadol alone –

on that scale,
this is a solid eight

the doctor stares at me
for a moment

we don't usually deal
with this kind of injury, he says
you know, muscular things,

there are places
i can refer you

with my second child, i say,
i didn't even bother asking
            for pain relief

ii

at pick-up, another mother
at my daughter's school
tells me she had
the exact same thing

that every time she took a step,
it felt like the ground was burning

she sends me to her osteo

by then, the pain is almost at a nine,
and i am willing to try anything

linda's osteo
has a new machine
that is going to shoot ultrasound waves
        deep into the soles of my feet

it might hurt a little, he says,
this machine has only recently become
available to public practitioners

before that, it was utilised in sports medicine:
it applies a light trauma to the area,
to stimulate blood flow,
and trick the body
        into accelerated healing

he kind of ... strokes the machine,
like it's his favourite
shiny new thing

linda's osteo's
shiny new machine
is like an electric hammer
against the nerves in my feet

hurts so bad
that for several minutes,
i cannot even collect myself
        to speak

relax your calves,
        the osteo says

you'll get used to it,
after a couple treatments

iii

i google podiatrists,
around the suburb where i live;

pick the first clinic
on an easy bus route

he's young –
early thirties, at a guess:
speaks plainly, wears kind eyes
atop his black–and–white adidas tracksuit

the podiatrist doesn't ask me
what is the walking stick for,
why didn't you come earlier,
or *can you rate your pain*
on a scale of one to a panadol-birth

he asks, *how many sessions*
of the ultrasound did you have,
trying not to look shocked

there haven't really been
any clinical trials
to prove the efficacy
of that kind of treatment

then, sensing my discomfort, he says
but, i know how it is:

if it hurts enough,
you try anything

he asks how far i walk
on a daily basis

i walk my daughter
to school and back,
the one-way trip is about
two kilometres, so eight

he turns his head, to stare
at the walking stick

when he turns back,
his eyes don't meet mine

sometimes,
a neighbour stops
and gives us a lift,
i say, weirdly defensive

the podiatrist
notes down my lack of health cover,
but lets me know
he'll do everything he can

before we think about how to fix
whatever's causing this,
       the nice podiatrist says,
we just need to get rid
of some of the pain

you can't be
living like this

he runs strapping tape
at one-inch intervals,
down the length and width
of both my feet

the tape
holds the muscles
the way they should sit,

and pulls back the hurt
to around about a six

next time, he says,
i want you to bring in one shoe,
from each pair of shoes
you regularly use

i sleep that night,

held together
with sticky plaster,

painkiller-free,

for the first time
in weeks

iv

three visits in,
the podiatrist refers me
to his colleague

the physiotherapist
in the next room

the physio
is the kind of guy
who made the smart kids' lives
hell, back in high school

tells me straight up
i am carrying
too much weight,
and that's probably
          part of the problem

asks me to climb
on the fat-measuring machine,
and when my ratio
is not nearly what he anticipated,

doesn't even have the decency
to appear ashamed

the physio hands me
five-kilo weights

the podiatrist said i shouldn't
do anything load-bearing, i say

trust me on this, the physio grins

as the ten extra kilos
travel slowly down my body,
and splay the tender muscles
in the arches of my feet

v

the nice podiatrist phones
several times

just checking in,
noticed you missed
your physio appointment,

trouble walking

when you have a moment,
please give me a call

i hear the worry in his voice:
we were making progress, and
he wants to know
what went wrong

i wish i had the energy
to explain

thank you, genuinely,
for everything you did

i never came back
because the intersecting oppressions
of race and gender

mean your colleague
might permanently
                    injure me

vi

i learn to strap my aching feet,
from a tutorial on youtube

and do the strengthening exercises
the nice doctor ran me through

they never heal
the way i'd hoped

but eventually,
i walk without the stick

speculum

anarcha is seventeen

afro-curl tucked
beneath servant's bonnet,

as she cowers
on the surgeon's table

dr j. marion sims
is standing over her

and in the foreground
two of his colleagues,
with rolled-up
meaning-business sleeves

are readying to hold her down,
while the good doctor does his thing

in the painting,
anarcha's sister-slaves,
lucy and betsey, who know
all too well what lies ahead,

speculum

peek, terrified,
from behind a flimsy
          white privacy curtain

you can't tell
from thom's painting

that j. sims operated
on anarcha's vaginal fistulas
a minimum
          of thirty times

that her owner
consented

what use, after all,
was a female slave
          who could not bear?

the price her future children
          might fetch

speculum

well worth the risk
of operating, or death

in nineteenth-century montgomery,
at a time before anaesthetic

i wish she knew, anarcha:
some tiny consolation

for the indignity, the
terror, the excruciating pain

that at just seventeen,
screaming and ostracised,
brutalised and afraid

the mother
of modern
gynaecology

is who she
became

weight

they'll spin you this
and spin you that

about backyard butcher botch jobs,
coathanger clumsiness,
and girls just like you:

wearing baggy sweaters
to conceal their carry

giving birth
          in some high school bathroom

letting that tiny babe turn blue

because what else
          is a girl
from a god-fearing hail-jesus family
gonna even do

they'll sing of way back
before women had rights

and neighbourhood girls,
jumping high:

double-dutching
off kitchen tables
        to bring about their blood

or climbing the stairs
to give desperation
a mighty shove

cause don't no brown girl wanna show
like that big-belly-jane down the block

whose own mama
can't even say her name:
ain't not a one of us wanna live
        with that kind of shame

you got choices now, though, sweetie,
the white sister will smile,
writing the appointment up

what none-a them
women's rights campaigners
wanna tell you is:

us brown girls
didn't need no placards
for them not to want *us* to have kids

ever since we got free,
we were right up front the line
      for this

if you a brown gal

with an empty fridge
and scuffed shoes,
then places like this were built
especially for girls like you

for slum-queen ghetto-trash
brown gals with no man
or a where-he-gone man
or, to be honest,
any brown man at all

for girls like you,
with the getting-big-belly blues

see, marie stopes et al
they just moved in:
set up in our neighbourhoods,
these rich white-girl doctors
in crisp white coats
straight outta eugenics labs

and fancy medical schools

saying *you don't have to worry anymore*
you've got a choice now, we'll take care of you

help us snuff the future,
but they weren't so worried
about getting us the vote

want your body back

too young
don't got no money, or
didn't love him anyway

your family don't know, and
besides, how you think you're
gonna feed it anyhow?

so here you are sister,
here you are

ain't no backyard butcher botch job
or coathanger clumsiness, no baggy
sweaters to conceal your carry, or giving birth
in some high school bathroom:

fear balled in your fists
as that tiny babe turns blue

      nah

it's just *history*,
and you

iron

my friend warns me
       she had to fight
to get her hysterectomy

doctors don't like
to take organs out,
       if they feel like
they don't have to

especially, you know,
with women

you mean
with white women,
i think, but
       i don't say anything

i am here
for the anaemia

for months,
i have been having
iron transfusions

could be
the fibroids
the x-ray showed,

in any case,
they need to take a look

we could think about
taking everything out,

      the doctor says,
you know, if you've finished
having children

then it won't be something
you have to come back for

      it's just all dusted
      and done

muscle memory

they say communities of colour
are the worst affected
in this pandemic

that they catch it at a faster rate, get sicker
when they do, have more co-morbidities, and
a higher ratio of death, display more extreme
vaccine suspicion, and are far less likely
                    to seek medical help

what they don't say is

communities of colour are
working in the nursing homes, are cleaning and staffing
hospital wards, make food in the kitchens
of healthcare spaces,
are disposing of infected bodies and toxic medical waste,
that because of economic disparity, we are more likely
to live in cramped or difficult living situations
where it is almost impossible
                    that disease will not spread

communities of colour remember
the tuskegee experiment: that
just shy of four hundred black sharecroppers
          were deliberately infected with syphilis:
left to go blind, to die,
to lose their minds

we have not forgotten

communities of colour were given
smallpox-infected blankets, we remember
how henrietta lacks' cells
were harvested without permission

that beyond hospital doors

our babies die faster, our mothers
don't make it, we are given less pain relief, have
worse medical and operation outcomes
and, are at a higher risk,
of almost any kind
                    of death

communities of colour *know*

that yesterday,
before our wellbeing
could be tangibly tied
                    to theirs

they really didn't give a fuck

whether or not
we lived

THE
BLOOD-
TRUTH

hotel alice

on march 21
the people's feet thundered,

seven thousand,
through the township
  of sharpeville

chanting *izwe lethu*:

come hell or mandela,
they would fell the passbook laws

sixty-nine dead

without one
  dispersion warning

wailing children carried the bodies
of wailing children carried
their mothers shouldered
      the men

and all the black and
fertile soil,

  sunken with their blood

we call it *harmony day*,
down here,

    in the land
where apartheid still exists

and the laws of apartheid
                            began

home to biloela

it chilled the blood,

      it felt different, this time,
when the deportation vans arrived

they lived next door
and were just like us:

he worked the abattoir
(bloody tough)

the wife: smiling away
   when her trolley passed yours

always stopped for a chat
        and said g'day

in the cereal aisle
down the iga

and their little girls,
they were sunshine rays

shit,

     our kids'd been over their house
to play

couldn't have taken nicer people
's what all the biloela locals'd say

it feels different, this time:

this whole town,
        we watched that family

grow

the little one
toddling down at the park

barefoot, and cheeky,
and always laughing

across the coarse green buffalo

for the love of god,
it feels different, this time,

we can't send them back,

                we *know* them

surveillance

the blood-truth is:

it's much less about the camera,
and much more to do with the body

that it's worn on

the body with the baton
hanging from its belt, the body
blue, the body on the cop beat,
clenching fists around a point-blank
pepper-spray can, the body
who holds the rein, that rears the riot
horse, the body trained

to wield

       the gun

 it is conviction-clear now,

    what most of us knew
two years ago,
when the *surveillance devices act*
    was amended

back then,
victoria police said
bodycams would be
the third eye:

that there was
nothing to worry about,
       and importantly,

this would ensure that officers
do the right thing

but we all knew

we knew
that it was not the people
who needed watching

that those cameras only shoot
from the same angle
as the coppers do:

no matter who does what, no matter
what goes down,

that device
can only ever be pointed

    at you

victoria police,
they brought in bodycams

    and they now admit
they have the power

to edit or delete

trust them,
they will only do it *sparingly*

meanwhile, bystanders' smartphones
capture disproportionate force:
midway through an episode
headlocked hard against the asphalt

concerned for his own welfare, and
he'd called for help himself

meanwhile, neighbours say
nah, it never went down like that:

their guns were cocked
before anyone even answered
the door

had he really skipped parole,
or was it just supposed to be
        a routine check-up call

where were bodycams then:
we have heard it all before

the blood-truth is,

it's much less about the gun
        and much more to do with the body
that it's trained on:

the body with the placard
raised in fist, the body-brown,
the body-colonised, the body
of a struggling mind

the body easy
to get away with beating:

clenching eyelids against a point-blank
pepper-spray can, the body underneath
the rearing riot horse, the body well trained

to fear
the blue

wolf pack

they say he was *a lone wolf*:

wreaked blood-carnage
in a black church in charleston

they say he was *a lone wolf*:
that butter-wouldn't-melt bowl-cut blond boy

who came friendly-in
        with a mock-shy smile
right on bible-study time,

and opened fire

they say he was *a lone wolf*:
heavy-breathing, hunting the halls
at marjory stoneman douglas high

a lone wolf who drew swastikas
        on the gun magazines,

in the worst upper-school massacre
of all united states time

a lone white wolf
killed hispanics this week, in el paso

a lone wolf
massacred muslims,
in christchurch, last march

they say *a lone white wolf*
killed seventy-seven,
        on an island in norway

a lone wolf
shot up the synagogue,
down in pittsburgh

say *a lone white wolf*
in london vehicle-rammed
the finsbury park mosque

these *lone wolves*

wolf pack

defy all sense, analysis
and logic

just who or what
could have made them this way

 if only we knew

but they are *lone wolves*
 you understand

so we don't ever
see them coming

 until after they do

nineteen

and by the end,
no one dared to say his name

so we called him
     nineteen

because of how they said
it all began

that nineteen votes
let a man into the halls of parliament
who invoked the crimes of nuremberg

whose words caught
round the necks of folk of colour

   and contracted, like rope

   they told us
nineteen votes let a man to lead
who tabled white supremacy

and on whose hate
the angry dark-webbed corners
then would feed

they said *nineteen*

   senatored a man
whose kind of tongue, some say, inspired the minds
that ruled the hands that loaded ar-15s
   and who would kneel amongst the slaughter
laying blame on the beloved-innocent,
   like wreath

so in the end,
   when we could not say his name

we said

     nineteen

the last post

my mother would wake us
well before dawn

our shoes were shined,
our hair was cornrowed

the car rough-starting,
        in the cold morning air

as mum popped the boot
for the large black case
of my older sister's bass clarinet

for weeks, our school concert band
had been rehearsing
        let there be peace on earth

on anzac day
the old men with medals
didn't stare, or tut-tut
        like that time we went for dinner
at the local rsl

the last post

on anzac day, they smiled,
and patted my head:

the negro trumpet girl

lenticular cloud
for grieving christchurch

across the tasman,
through a westerly,

    in ōtautahi, aotearoa,

land of the long

      white

cloud,

lives a tiny creature:
warbling, flightless

unlike any
    endothermic vertebrate

the great spotted kiwi
loves for a lifetime

when she bears,
she lays a higher ratio
for her size

    than any other

to bring new life
to bring new life

to ōtautahi, aotearoa

COMMUNION

COMMUNION

royal

folktale has it
        new arrivals,
they'll throw any queen
or kingdom
        into spin:

angered uninvited guests
will conjure curses

horses are saddled,
messengers dispatched far and wide
to burn the spinning wheels

firstborns, golden,
they are worth their wait:

their christened names
secreted away

        lest rumpelstiltskin hear
the whispers

so, the sussex baby's here:

son of an english prince,
and in his lineage slaves

son of a proud black kween,
and in his lineage masters

the empire has new clothes,
           that's what i hear

cause in the end,
           the baby's just a baby:
bringing all the soiled nappies,
gummy-smiling, chucking, waking nights
and charming,

   even while in tears

no more royalty
than any other born that day,

and no less wonder

that true love
has brought to bear

liber pauperum

on the western facade
    the archangel michael,
grand wings aloft,
was weighing souls

and the serpent hissed down
    at eve, regal,
and adam

as thomas the apostle
put a hand
        to his brow

and ash-wind dusted
    the upturned faces
as bystanders wide-eyed
the hellfire blaze

the cathedral spire
    skeleton, blackened:
a falling splendour
of gothic past days

and smoulder plumed
        like anger, woken:

like a strength immortal
emerged from the tomb

and oh, the screams of the people
atheistic,
    and praying,

and the spectacle smarted
the eyes of the world

oh, notre dame
oh, liber pauperum:

the carved poor people's book
of illiterate stone

and the smoke, it rose spiral
like sacrament incense:

    a purging,
like the faithful
    ascending above

eight short days
before easter sunday

118

when the skies of paris,
ochre-scarlet, lit up

but perhaps the church burned
like no second coming;

like cult of reason,
not latin rite

like falling empire,
    and the sins of the clergy,

and the power of the people

révolution française

section 116

in grade eleven, our legal studies teacher
fired up the overhead projector

 and fuzzy grey handwriting was cast
        on the classroom wall

the constitution:
separation of church and state,
section 116

                and finally, i felt seen

the exclusive brethren had a church,
in the suburb where i grew

the brethren kids coloured in next to us
        at the local primary school

the girls wore scarves and ribbons
on waist-length plaits, the boys
were pleat-ironed straight
                down the leg
of their trouser king gees

they didn't play with us heathens

suburban summertimes sucking orange
zooper doopers, bright green bullrush
chasing-game-stains smudged across
                    our kmart sandshoes

my dad went door to door with a petition, once:
something about a dangerous bridge

that more than half the town wanted closed

they were very polite, the brethren folk:
said they couldn't sign
    with nonbelievers,
but they'd write one of their own

they didn't like politics,
        or voting,
(but dad said they bankrolled
        some parties to win)

brethren homes, they were easy to spot:
it was a game we played, my siblings and me

federation-style; lots of wood detailing,
and no aerial on the roof for a tv

mum said they didn't like *modern things*

and they were strange,
      but then apparently,
 so were we

walking home, neighbourhood kids
      trailed long sticks
along corrugated fences
thunkerrthunkerrthunk

      but we always avoided theirs

mostly, they just *were*
but sometimes, the adult townsfolk
gave them a wide berth

like on friday nights

      when they grouped together
outside *nick's fish and chips,*
and yelled about us going to hell

repent to the lord, sinners,
or you will burn for all eternity

thick leather bibles
held threateningly high
       above righteous heads

we were terrified, us kids

during scripture class,
the brethren kids were *excused*

they played cat's cradle
outside on the balcony

i wanted to be *excused* too

   you don't have a god,
scoffed the weird wild-eyed
volunteer lady, who
came every week, to teach us jesus
   and you need something to believe in

i always hope i'll see her,
when i visit home

i'd ask her what she means

because it's still *something*,
what i believe in:

kindness and tolerance,
generosity, and truth,

our innate capacity
to be good to each other,

                    and section 116

things about dying

in my home state, now, by law
    those leaving us can tread gently:
usher themselves towards the light

in the dignity they see fit

and i can't remember all of their names,
they and i were strangers,
    but when i heard,
i thought of them

like the kind-eyed man
on the second floor:
slight form wasting
    beneath thin hospital sheets

every morning smiling-hopeful,
saying *lass, today might be the day*

week after week,
    drawing back from the pain:
turning away,
    as i quietly brought the breakfast
tray in

my friends and i
we were all gonna be somebody,

back then

every one of us had a hustle, to an end

me, i worked the hospital kitchen
to fund the degree

eight hours a day on your feet, hotplate
burns, clocked meal breaks, industrial
dishwashers that could take hands off (and once
did), two-hundred-kilo trolleys to push six-days-on
three-days-off, november to march, from age
eighteen to twenty-three

it got me here

but i know things about dying
that would haunt your dreams

we were always the first to know,
     down in the plating room

we knew before the doctors did

when the little freckled girl
     with the bald head and crooked smile

left jelly off her order sheet

the leading hand that afternoon
was on salt, pepper and cutlery:

she yelled down the line, in a shaky voice

    no dessert for bed fourteen

nobody spoke for the rest of meal prep

and after the trolleys were loaded,
    she gave everyone a break

we went outside
    and passed round cigarettes

communion

and if hell exists

   hail mary, full of grace
then surely they have lived it

and
   hail mary, mother of god

there is a special place
inside rome's gates
for men like him

they say his shadows fall over communion
goblets his crisp white collars bleach
bed-wet horrors his
swishing long church robes

      conceal

 the sunday darkness

of which they
(children, shiny-shoed
and trembling)

dare not
dared not

   speak

but now they have

and
  hail mary, mother of mercy
give them strength
  hail mary, bring them peace
and oh
  hail mary, mirror of justice

we believe them,

      we *believe*

kneeling

a lot can go down
along the 200 red burning
   metres of track

between the victory lap
       and the starter gun

   on the podium,
tommie smith and john carlos
could bow their heads
   for civil rights,

and raise their proud black gloved fists
   all the way to the sun

kathrine switzer
   might register
under an assumed name
for the boston marathon

and just like that, line up
     with the men

   around half-time,
nicky winmar
or adam goodes

could remind us
      exactly whose land we're on

the afl might start a women's league,
and cricket teams could refuse to play

  until the UN
convenes

  to end
apartheid in sport

whether or not
they will stand

    for the anthem

may well be
what a world-class athlete
becomes known for

is the number on your back

    worth more

than how you ran
the team home
   to gold
in a thought-unwinnable
       4×100

which

     flag

do you fly

serena williams
might nonchalantly keep serving,
caster semenya may choose
   to run on

and all while the crowd brays,
kaepernick could keep kneeling

   and little things
could slowly change

the memory of your better half

it's a ten-year-old brown girl,
    already weary from the world at large,
somehow stumbling
upon a copy of maya angelou's

    and still i rise

understanding as she reads
    – yes, my honey dumpling –
for the very first time
that self-love, black love, *you* love

is the only way a child-girl-woman,

        person,

will get out of here
                alive

art

is the memory
of your better half:

fifteen glorious years together

she fought hard, but slipped away,
        after the first round
of radiation

it's the kids, the next morning,
staring at you, with fear written

on their tiny faces

like: *where's our mama gone,*
you don't know how to make french toast
much less do our braids

art is six months after that,

        when you're through the worst,
and your song comes on the radio

this time, it makes you smile, though:

her, in that hot pink dress,
twirling to the chorus, all the way

down the aisle,

        and how her blunt fringe

134

brushed your shoulder,
after she kissed you
and became your wife

it's how the harmony makes you *feel*,
as you're folding the school clothes
the way *she* would have liked

    art
is the closest
one can get
to god

and in fact, exactly what it means
    to have a soul

art is at the heart
of all that we are

the markings on the wall,
and who walked here,
and everything that came before

who cares, thinks the prime minister,
where we stick art, in the portfolios of the nation:
it's not about coal power, or
curbing welfare, or wealth generation

here is a man
not nearly enlightened enough
   to understand
how closely they are linked:

that painting gives pennies back to medicare, that
old-time jazz, that opera, eases congestion
in the hospitals, helps our old folk live
longer in their own homes, that cultural
and creative activity pumps more than one hundred
billion dollars into our economy,

that poetry
       is why that kid so close to falling
through the cracks
           even gets up
and walks to school, that
sometimes the books in the library
are the only good place you have to go,

and there is nothing else on earth
like the hushed leaning-forward-together crowd

as bangarra dances
another show

A STARTING
WAGE

fourteen and nine months

and we were all waiting
for that golden age,
      of fourteen and nine months,
and a starting wage

a paper route, stacking shelves at franklins,
or working checkout at the safeway

sweeping salon floors at the local mall
(that was me, circa 1994)

couple months in, mum said
      what's the pay?

and i knew it was bad
by the look on her face
      begged her *please don't call the boss*
but she was mum,
and she did it anyway

next weekend, the salon fell silent

as i slunk in, ashamed,
      past offcut curls, and
dirty bleach trays, into the staffroom
to put my backpack away

cold-shouldered for two hours,
they'd forgotten they hated me
by midday

that weekend,
my yellow pay envelope
contained $6.20 an hour,
and time and a half
      for the sunday

it felt like a gift,
what was rightfully mine

i was there for twelve months,
and never got the back pay

there is a mastertheft happening
somewhere in australia

every second of every day

a small-hearted *self-made* man
is made big, by the workers
      he chooses not to pay

and it's *always* an accident,
and an oversight, and an underpayment

the law lets walk
the seven-million-dollar men
who steal the wages
        of working australians

and even then, we hear the bray

for unwieldy sanctions
on the union folk
who fight to save them:
    batting for the kids
without mothers like mine,
and grown-ups just happy to *have* a job,

cause we all know what happened
to the last kitchen hand
who dared to whine:

unpaid overtime is saving the industry:
if you don't fucken like it,
give the apron to me

fourteen and nine months

there's a new lot behind you
we're happy to pay

and they're ready at the pass

of that golden age,

fourteen and nine months,
and a starting wage

bridge

i

never thought you'd end up here
nah, not you

with *people like this*

we are all just one small disaster
away from sinking,

and sometimes you only realise
when you're gasping for air

what happened,

that our hearts are no longer
big enough

to take us there

didn't have a mental illness
until you did

three small and stoic kids;
boss said there was no safety harness
just an hour before you slipped

the redundancies
came out of fucking nowhere

mama had a fall;
no money for the nursing home
and you couldn't do that anyway

nah, not to her

sometimes a handout *is* a hand up,
that's the thing

and it's never you

it's never you,
until it is

and so what,
and god bless you,
if it never hits

cause rorting pollies with investment houses
and lifetime pensions that we'll all pay
will flood the airways screaming
     empathy is not the way

they'll find the haystack-few who work
the system, and round them up,
bowed-headed, to parade

and god forbid

god forbid
you're accidentally
overpaid

nah, not your fault

but at forty dollars
till the cupboard empties
a robocall is all that stands
between packing lunches

     and an early grave

we are all one

bridge

automated
debt-collect
away

ii

caught skint,
at the iga counter

frantic hands searching threadbare jeans
sorry, guess i'm short on change today
forgot my card

as you put the tampons,
the washing liquid and
your pride
                away

weighed down by life,
and weighing up

between bread, milk
bananas, nappies for the baby

more have lived it
than would care to say:
that's the thing, isn't it,
about cultivating shame

and is it not
what welfare means:
the happiness, health,
or fortunes of a group;
a social effort, designed to promote
the basic wellbeing of people in need

somewhere along the line,
it came to mean *greed*

saying things like *stop-gap*
and *it's not meant to be permanent, anyway*

but the damage, that's permanent:
there are *always* things that stay

the sheer heart-weight of every time you said
nah, i already ate today,
        ladling out to the kids, your mum, the flatmate
or your lover, the last
        of the bolognaise

knowing they know that you know
that they know you're lying,
that's what stays

and all the nights you lie awake

cause the new place is so close to the highway
you can hear the windows shake

printer's broken down, library's four k away
need to print your résumé,
the pair of shoes you have will get you there

but might not hold together
for the interview on wednesday

you don't shake that off,
when you finally get a job;

the knowing you'll die sooner
from red ink on bills

and it's harder for hungry children
to learn nine times tables

the indignity,
that's what stays:

the failure

standing in the job-find line
day after day, hoping
no one who knows you hears,
    as they loudly call your name

what stays
are the smug looks
of men in suits

who earn more
    than a fortnight *stop-gap*
in a single day

as you're begging them,
as you're begging them,

to *raise the rate*
raise the rate

of those who'll live
to tell the tale

banking day

wednesdays were banking day

grubby-faced kids in pleat-legged pants
        or red-checked tunics
shoved chubby fistfuls of
bronze coins
        into little yellow passbooks

and the teacher
would collect the savings basket

heavy with mowed lawns, and washed dishes,
and helping dad fix the car

we were the dollarmite generation

        we saw paper notes withdrawn
and found dull fifty-cent pieces
under pilled couch cushions, we
ransacked mum's messy glove box
and nanna's top drawer

        cashed in plastic bottles and aluminium cans
collected down the park

rounded careful numbers
on perforated deposit slips

we were the boomer kids of the boomer kids,
taught that everything good
     was worth waiting for

new cabbage patch dolls, pogo sticks,
matchbox cars
were always
   just another nine cents ahead

last monday was banking day:

the findings of the royal commission
came in:

a thick dossier of broken hopes
and damning testimony
to the lies
   that we believed

we are the dollarmite generation

the new car, apartment,
laptop, renovation
is always
        just another loan away

we are the round careful numbers
in the royal commission pages:

thin-shirted and red-eyed behind
poker machines, begging smiling tellers
cut me off, cut me off please

then mailed out
a new credit increase

we are the boomer kids of the boomer kids

we hold our parents' hands through chemo
        as they're buried before time

and the banks up tax
on whatever's left behind

we are sobbing, selling up, overcharged, begging
        for more time
to save face
to save our homes, our jobs
our dreams and reputations
and what little left we have to leave
the boomers of the boomers
of the boomer generation

wednesdays are banking day:

and our children
fold eager plastic notes
in black banking passbooks

waiting for their teacher
        to collect the savings basket

david

we remember
how they felled

      the giants

back when working childbirth
was a let-down into lactose-stained uniform,
sobbing as you fixed your hair,
heart sighing,
and a howling babe in arms
      every leaving morning

     union thugs
got our working mothers
twelve newborn months at home

not a dollar,
or a day longer,

    but at least a job on their return

we remember

how pilbara stockmen walked off, how coal
workers galvanised, how shearers

downed their tools, the migrant workers
who broke the factory line

> out at broadmeadows ford

tired of no-break pay-dock
disrespect, and falling ill
from their sweatshop
dusk-till-dawn

how straight-backed cops
charged their bucking horses
into picket lines

but the car-parts workers
stood their ground

> *union thugs all*
> *union thugs all*

david

we remember,
how we watched

goliath

fall

FIRE MOVES FASTER

fire moves faster

for 2020, the year that was

i

south of the equator

the summer
that set the year on fire
        was combustible:

the cotton sweat-slick of shirt-to-back

air so humid, the world turned
in slow motion

far-flung ash, settling to dust
on grimy city windowsills

the sour smell of singed flesh
drifting on the wind
        as wild things, whimpering
padded scorched and tender feet
towards outstretched bottles
        of volunteer mount franklin

the summer that lit the year that was
        flew magpies, so traumatised

in their mimicry
they wailed like sirens:

indistinguishable
from death's call

january was dark smoke,
        spreading in the distance

all kinds of folk glanced up
as they boarded the tram to work, got
the lawnmower out, hung the washing, took
a break from their word doc, or bunged
the team coffee pot on
saying *jesus, mate, look at that sky*
you just know it can't be good

february was small-town apple-eyed folk:
faces tear-tracked, and
racked with hiccup-sobs
on the early evening news

as they stared down the barrel
of abc rural

smouldering, amongst the embers
of all they thought they knew

by march, catastrophe
had leapt the break

collecting up sticks, seed pods, dry grass
and brittle undergrowth

anything was tinder:
                    whatever would take

ii

news out of china
was street spray-downs
and hazmat suits

          there were clips circulating
of officials brute-handling
those who broke
         the isolation rules

we heard tell of mask mandates
and the harsh seal of infected citizens
into their own rooms

watching from below the equator
it seemed strange-apocalyptic,
      what was happening
in wuhan

at first, we thought the virus
was unknown quantity,
then they said they had named it

covid-19

in march, it ravaged italy
and we saw, my god,
just what this virus meant to do:

saw morgues too full to take
the bodies on trolleys, lining the walls
of hospital hallways, rasping beneath
thin standard-issue sheets, and the doctors

and nurses
        well, they were dying too

looking back, italy
was the moment
we all *knew*

that something wicked
this way wandered

fire burns faster, when
travelling uphill

the virus slipped in on unwashed
airport hands at melbourne international,
the virus hitched a ride in the eager lungs
of working cruise-ship youngsters, the virus
nonchalantly dropped anchor
        in the new south wales ports

to some, it was nothing
compared to what arrived
        two hundred and fifty years before

we knew the fever, the
shadow-on-lung; the way
it broke the body down

but what we never really thought about
was how we'd watch
our loved ones
                    die alone

how bone-tired nurses would hold ipads
to their faces; and do their fearful best to show
despite the empty room, the face shields,
the absence of any human touch for days

they were thought about
and they were loved, and
there were people who prayed

some lauded that the virus could hunt you down
no matter who you were, no matter
where you lived, no matter
what you earned

but that was back before factory workers
were put off, before one hundred days

of lockdown, before well-to-do folk
bought the supermarkets out of
toilet paper, canned goods,
hand sanitiser and meat

before chemists had no emergency flixotide left
          and none available to order
for your asthmatic kid

and chain hardware stores sold out
of veggie seeds, and whitegoods places
had a run on deep freezers

before they sealed
the public housing towers up
and we saw the brown
– and rightly angry – faces
staring down at us
from hundredfold windows
          as they trucked in one cop
to every five residents

and in reality: nobody quite knew,
or cared, what the real infection numbers were
out of india, or brazil

while some of us queued for food, and housing,
celebrities broadcast themselves singing
                              imagine

arty news crews shot
footage of cherubic choirboys
singing in the centres of empty cities;
took poignant stills
of playgrounds closed off with cautionary tape;
newspapers ran pics of small children
pressing heartbroken hands against
grandma's window-peeking face

on the first day of online learning
my hopeful daughter
wore her uniform

        to the kitchen table

iii

may arrived,
and on a daylight street
in minneapolis, minnesota

a swagger-cocky white cop
knelt on the neck
of an unarmed black man
          for more than nine minutes

until he ceased to breathe

in may, george floyd
          was asphyxiated

by callous knee of an officer, by
cruel might of state, and
under crushing weight of colony

george floyd was run down
by the slave hounds that never stopped
lifting wet noses, sniffing the air
to smell our blood;
          never stopped snarling
at black folk's heels

when george floyd cried *mama, mama*
when george floyd said *i can't breathe*

every black child-bearer
   and every black child
heard their own child cry for mercy

saw through centuries; felt the lick
of overseer's whip, splitting proud black skin
felt the sharp, and weeping smart
of plum-red flesh, the desperation
       and indignity

fire travels faster
when burning uphill

but june came the strength
of proud black people
june came the fervour
   of our righteous rage

in bristol, protesters sunk a cast
of edward colston in the harbour

in washington, they almost
   tore andrew jackson down

in ghent, king leopold II was
doused in paint
the crimson colour
          of congo artery

oh, the streets were awash
with black and yellow
june was a march of red
                    and green

black lives matter
black lives matter

in australia, the press gave more space
to deaths in custody

for just a moment
you could taste a dream

later, in october,
as the melbourne lockdown
                         lifted

they would quietly fell
a djab wurrung tree

iv

in victoria, during the first wave,
it kind of became ritual:

the premier, standing before the press,
and the people, crowded around their
home tv sets,
         jostling to hear

when you think about it deeply,
it kind of sung of war:

on saturdays and sundays,
the premier wore north face

and on weekdays, a signature dark suit

the chief health officer, *brett*,
soon garnered a cult following

the pin-ups of 2020 could rock a statistic

some looked hot in both heels
and health policy
could pull off that lab coat scientist-chic

you couldn't meet for tinder dates,
but all the swipe-rights
designed contact-tracing systems
        in their sleep

get yourself a bae who can hook up a ventilator,
but will wash up their coffee cup too

lanky teens stacking
supermarket aisles
            on thursday nights
had more certain employment
than the dentists did

in some ways
the new status quo
was delightfully. fucking. weird.

the world was a trash fire
but it was all avoidable:

your kid's playdate after school with
that child you think is a *terrible influence*;
        book club with jenny,
who insists on chewing jatz
with her mouth
                   wide open

that pap smear you got a reminder for
two months ago
i mean, it's selflessness really: can't go now,
wouldn't want to clog up the medical system

the courage to quit that job
that's been giving you stress-eczema
for going on a year

you could pocket jobkeeper:
netflix and uber eats while you wait
and who even knows,
          maybe there'll be redundancy pay

introducing your new partner
to your dad and mum

yeah, nah, sorry,
we're all in lockdown
i mean, i do wish we could come

routine was tuning in
between ten am and one

to check out
what was happening
          with the curve

pollies and journos spun their usual crap:

that tim smith, down state,
who can never shut up
          at the best of times
was always mouthing off
about *daniel andrews* this
and *daniel andrews* that

and rachel baxendale
from the murdoch press
tied up
          every covid conference
with tedious *i-got-you*'s

175

berejiklian got involved
with some real shady-arse bloke

it was like:
>   *sister, just ... nope*

the prime minister fucked up
trade deals, left and right:
souring diplomatic ties
like a small, stubborn child

spent the rest of his time
courting votes
>   and singing hillsongs

no matter what happens,
>   *politics* rolls on

v

planes were grounded, motorcars
slept street-side, birds
repopulated silent cities

some said the upside was
they had never breathed
air so clean

but trauma
does not reverse
so easily

a tornado ripped through sumatra,
taal erupted in the philippines;
bush-burn raged through colorado and california
        through faulconbridge and northmead

the atlantic
ran out of the english alphabet

when christening hurricanes
this season

fire travelled faster,
when roaring uphill

vi

by november,

washington
was a sea of white flags

each solemn-planted
for one of the dead

when election rolled round
the early voters
queued the block

exit polls showed
it was largely black women
                and native american voters

who stood up, and shouted out,
and in united numbers
                got the job done

president trump tried every avenue
to beat them back, but the
roads were all painted
with *black lives matter*

the victory, well, it wasn't much
but it was also just enough

fire travels faster,
when climbing up

for a moment, we forgot the pandemic
and the floods, and the shootings
and the blasts, forgot to wonder
where next month's rent
would be coming from

and the whole world stood
       and watched, in awe

as decent americans
packed city street-sides, singing mariah carey
from subwoofed rides, as they formed
philadelphian street parades, as
chicago fireworks shone
       and flash mobs were made,
as harlem hodge-podged
marching bands,

and new york crowds
made cool jazz hands

the whole world stood
  and watched, in awe

and the united states
of america

partied its way
to a brand-new dawn

vii

sometimes,

you don't wanna
think too much
about the year that was,
 you know

the 1.6 million empty places
at the kwanzaa, the hanukkah
and the christmas table

the elders you'll skype,
  cause you still can't meet

the lockdown weight
so many still carry

all the small, and poignant, ways
we couldn't help but have to change

how you scrub your hands
            a little too hard
these days,
at the bathroom sink

how,
        most nights,
despite going to bed early,
you still don't get much sleep

the handful of emergency cans
you now insist on keeping

and the flinch,
when some stranger brushes by,

the distance between us,
and how readily you cry

there is hope, in little things

watching the zucchini plants flower,
sharing a meal with friends

loud children,
playing tag in the park again

realising you know
your neighbour's name

how a mass of screaming bodies,
worldwide, on city streets,
can harness the voice
        of an entire people

what a city can overcome

what ordinary people
will muster to give

how *fire moves faster,*
when travelling uphill

and how fiercely we realised
how fiercely we realised

we all will fight, to live

ACKNOWLEDGEMENTS

Thank you, first and foremost, to my family, for supporting my writing journey – particularly Mali and Maya, for being great lockdown-mates during a lot of the time this collection was being written. Thanks to Ernest, for endlessly listening to me rail about the chaos around us, while I wrote about the chaos around us. Thank you to the good folks at Hachette Australia, for taking the leap into poetry with me again – in particular Fiona Hazard, Sophie Mayfield, Layla Saadeldine, Louise Stark and Madison Garratt. My eternal gratitude to Ali Lavau, for your sharp editing eye, and Allison Colpoys for the stunning cover design – it's an honour to once again have my words so beautifully dressed by you. And thanks to Robert Watkins, for seeding this book by publishing my last poetry collection, *Carrying the World*.

Early versions of some of the poems in *How Decent Folk Behave* were published by *The Saturday Paper*, during my time writing as the paper's Poet Laureate. Thanks to Michael Nolan, Maddison Connaughton, Ian See, Cindy MacDonald and Erik Jensen for their editorial work on these pieces. And to fellow poets Ellen van Neerven, Omar Sakr and Paul Kelly for being part of the poetry team that once was – and their words.

The poem *my feminism* was commissioned by the Victorian Women's Trust, for International Women's Day 2017. The poem *weight* was first published in the anthology *Choice* (Allen & Unwin, 2019). The poem *grace* was commissioned by ABC Online, and first published in May 2020.

Thank you to all the poets, poetry readers and poetry pushers I've read and met on this journey. To choose poetry, again and again, set up against the world that is, truly requires the faith-absolute and the fire-brilliant. To Black poets everywhere, our words matter.

Maxine Beneba Clarke is the author of the Victorian Premier's Literary Award-winning poetry collection *Carrying the World*, the ABIA and Indie Award-winning short fiction collection *Foreign Soil*, the critically acclaimed childhood memoir *The Hate Race*, the *Boston Globe*/Horn Prize-winning picture book *The Patchwork Bike*, and several other books for adults and children. *How Decent Folk Behave* is her fourth poetry collection.